Cc

ISBN-13: 978-1731543257

TABLE OF CONTENTS

INTRODUCTION

For me, words are a form of action, capable of influencing change.—Ingrid Bengis

At any time in your life, you can achieve just about anything you want. If you feel the desire to learn music today, you can do that. If you want to learn to be a great cook, manager, writer or even an actor, it's all there within you. There is not a gene that is preventing you from creating success. All you need is the courage to dream and the will to make the dream a reality. Of course, you need to take charge and find the right tools (the purpose of this book) to put your mind to the test. The point is, though, you CAN do it, if you DESIRE it.

However, you may have learned at an early age that you can't do that. Maybe you learned that only a select few are destined to have the skills, success, and lifestyle the rest desire. Maybe you came to believe that painting the beauty of the human face or fashion photography is for the masters who have the right stuff or that athletic ability is something that can be developed only in people who are naturally gifted.

People who think this way have a fixed mindset. With a fixed mindset, you think that skills and talents are set in stone and that you either have them or you don't. You know what you can and cannot do, and very little can be done to improve your abilities and success. Your mind is closed to the possibility of improvement and growth. You feel you have plumbed the depths of your mind, and there's nothing worthwhile there.

Conversely, if you are like the millions of successful people who are living the lives they dream, you think otherwise. You have a growth mindset. You realize that you can develop skills and habits at any stage in life, regardless of previous experience. The path of growth, opportunity and success lies here.

The growth mindset that underlies this book states that you can enhance your talents and improve the quality of your life to a far greater extent than most people think. The mind or brain is not hard wired to be good at any one thing or another, like writing a play, drawing a picture, kicking a soccer ball, having social skills, or being successful. Some people certainly seem to exhibit these talents and habits naturally, but the rest of us can develop them if we so desire.

Although we have this amazing ability, our internal thoughts and beliefs can get in the way of our success. Our conscious thoughts and subconscious beliefs are powerful. They have the power to control how we think, how we feel, how we act, and more importantly, how we perceive ourselves and our abilities. If you want to change yourself and your life, therefore, first you have to change your thoughts and beliefs.

This is where self-talk comes in.

CHAPTER 1 – YOU AND YOUR SELF-TALK

We all have voices in our heads which talk to us on an almost constant basis. Our voices give us messages continually, and what they say to us affects us.—
Juliene Berk

All of us talk to ourselves. We all do it. More or less, whenever you think about something, you are talking to yourself.

Much of the time you are not aware of this self-talk because it takes place automatically. Right now, as you read these words, conversations circulate in your head. The topic could be this book or what you plan to do this weekend. Maybe the dialogue is about work, school, or friends. Whatever the topic, you are always thinking (and thus self-talking) and these thoughts flow constantly, like sand through an hourglass.

You do not consciously choose most of your self-talk. Although it appears as though you are choosing your inner dialogue, you are not. It is simply coming into your awareness. You don't control it; it is occurring on its own.

If you don't believe me, try to stop your self-talk. Notice that it doesn't stop. Suddenly you start thinking about not thinking and thinking about how to stop thinking or even why you can't stop thinking. Nonetheless, you are still thinking.

This might be a bit much to take in, but having your self-talk running like this is very useful to have. First, your self-talk helps you guide your decisions and actions. For example, when you step too close to the curb of a busy intersection, your inner voice will direct you to step back. When you don't want to get out of bed in the morning, your inner thoughts will nag you until you get up. I'm sure you've experienced this nagging. It will say *Get up. You better get up now, it's getting late. You don't want to be late for work and have the boss yelling at you, now do you*? The next thing you know, you're out of bed.

Second, your inner dialogue helps you evaluate options. For example, you could be staring at the dinner menu at your favorite restaurant and become aware of your inner voice saying things like: *Oh, the spaghetti looks good, but I had pasta for lunch. I am in the mood for something different. The surf and turf looks good too, but seems a bit pricey for my tastes. I know what I am going to get, chicken parmesan. That's it. That's what I want*. When you come across various options, your self-talk helps you evaluate them so you can come to a decision.

More importantly, your self-talk comes up to remind you of things. If you are rushing home from work, you might hear a voice surface and say *stop at the Laundromat to pick up the dry cleaning* or *don't forget about your son's baseball game this evening*.

As you can see, being able to tune in to your self-talk in these ways can be helpful.

In other ways (as is the focus here), your self-talk is your 24-hours-per-day personal critic. It's always there assessing everything you're doing. It lets you know when you've done something wrong, when you have made a mistake, or when you have crossed the line in some way. In many cases, this is also useful, as it acknowledges that you're off the mark and that you need to get back on track.

Sometimes, however, and for some people, this critic has a way of getting out of control. It might constantly throw insults and negativity into your consciousness. It might say that you are not cut out for certain things, that you will make too many mistakes, or that you'll fail.

Your self-talk may be even harsher. When you make a mistake, your self-talk will berate you, put you down, and call you derogatory names. When you have a hard time making positive changes in your life, it may bemoan what a worthless person you are and conclude that you'll never do anything right.

Most often these messages began as statements uttered by the people in your life when you were a child. They may have said something negative about you when your actions displeased them, or perhaps they had a habit of saying unkind things even when you didn't deserve it.

As painful as these experiences can be, your subconscious has a way of picking up where they left off. As a result, you continue to repeat the same negative messages to yourself over and over. If you listen carefully, you may hear their voice and hear the quote, something like, *you'll never amount to anything*. Other people's negative voices have a way of seeping in and becoming your inner voice

Although your self-talk is a useful tool, having it running out of control like this can be harmful—for several reasons.

For starters, your thoughts affect your emotions. So if you have self-talk thoughts running out of control in a negative manner, you're frequently going to feel bad about yourself. Perhaps you can remember instances when your mood seemed to shift dramatically for no apparent reason. You were feeling fine, and then suddenly you were angry, sad, or depressed. Most likely, unbeknown to you, your self-talk began moving in an unproductive direction, triggering corresponding emotions.

Moreover, having these types of voices and feelings running in the background can makes it hard to accomplish any task or goal. You are probably all too familiar with this. Think about a time in the past when you wanted to change your life in a positive way or when you wanted to try something new, but your self-talk came up and said things like, *Wait, I can't do that. Remember what happened last time*, or *What's the use, I always screw up anyway.* As if by magic, your inner voice turned into a self-fulfilling prophecy.

Lastly, when you allow these thoughts to run long enough, they start to become beliefs. You actually begin to believe that you are an incapable and unworthy person. As you will learn in the next chapter, when your self-defeating thoughts turn into self-defeating beliefs, it's over. These beliefs bind to you internally and make a lesser person of you. Even if you consciously know these statements are false, it doesn't matter. When they become accepted within your subconscious, they guide your decisions and actions as if they were true.

What's worse, the key beliefs you hold about yourself and your life continue to influence the general direction of all other self-talk you have. It's a cycle. Your beliefs influence your self-talk, and your self-talk reinforces your beliefs. For many people, this cycle becomes a way of life. They get caught in a downward spiral of negative self-talk that damages many aspects of their being.

Still, there is hope. You can break this cycle and guide your mind in a healthier, more positive direction. You can do this by interrupting your self-talk pattern. Although your self-talk is a habitual process that is running on its own, you can interrupt it. At anytime you want, you can stop the thought that berates you or puts you down, and you can replace it with something more positive and encouraging.

That is, if you have a habit of making mistakes and following the mistake with a statement like *I'm an idiot, I can't do anything right*, then the next time you make a mistake, interrupt the self-scolding with *I am smart, I do things right*, and notice the results that you get. If you have a tendency to say *I hate myself* a lot, disrupt the pattern with *I like myself*. Again, notice the reaction.

You have a choice—the choice to change your thoughts or to let the negative ones to keep running. By acting on the choice to change, not only do you reverse the cycle of reinforcing negative beliefs, but you tell your subconscious that you want to be guided in a different direction—a *better* direction. And you know what, your subconscious will follow suit. Your self-talk will trigger a way of thinking and feeling that will guide you in the direction of your words, whether the words speak of avoiding mistakes or liking yourself more.

If you do it long enough, this interrupting and replacing will in of itself become a habit. The more you do it, the stronger the habit will get. Eventually, your self-talk messages will become self-sustaining beliefs, which will support the changes you want to make automatically.

In fact, you will be astounded at the level of inner strength you gain from the process. The stronger you feel, the more easily you can manage your thoughts and feelings. The more you manage your thoughts and feelings, the stronger you get.

If this is a direction you want to go in your life, great. Let's go further.

CHAPTER 2 - SELF-TALK YOUR WAY TO SUCCESS

First say to yourself what you would be; and then do what you have to do.—Epictetus

In the last chapter you learned about your self-talk, the ongoing dialogue you have with yourself about everything from day-to-day occurrences to the challenges life throws at you. You also learned how much power your self-talk has to influence your life, whether positively or negatively.

In this chapter you will learn the many ways you can use self-talk to influence yourself positively and create the constructive changes you desire. You will learn, among other things, how you can use self-talk to:

• change limiting and self-defeating beliefs

• support behavior and habit change you want to achieve

• shift your focus and energy, in the moment, from the negative to the positive

Change Limiting, Self-Defeating Beliefs

The main application of self-talk is to change your limiting and self-defeating beliefs. When you change your beliefs about who you are and what you are capable of, you set the natural processes in motion to become the person you want to be and to live the life you want to lead. To explain how this works, it helps to understand how your mind operates.

The mind operates on two levels of awareness: the conscious and the subconscious. The conscious mind is the aware portion of the mind, the thinking mind. You are reading this book—thinking and analyzing the content of each sentence—with your conscious mind. As you read, your heart continues to beat, your food digests, you blink and you breathe. These processes take place undetected, below the level of consciousness. This is your subconscious mind.

The conscious/subconscious distinction is extremely important. Your body runs hundreds of errands at once without you having to think about them. How difficult would it be to read this book or have a conversation with a friend and still remember to breathe, pump your heart, and control the million other processes of which you are unaware? Without any conscious effort on your part, your subconscious carries out 99% of what goes on inside your mind and body.

In addition to controlling the anatomic functions of the body, your subconscious is a storehouse of information, otherwise referred to as memory. Stored within your subconscious memory bank are behaviors, habits, and **beliefs** you have been acquiring since birth. Here is the magical word again, *beliefs*. So what are beliefs?

Beliefs are thoughts that you think are true or accept as self-evident. For example, *the Earth is round* is a thought you believe to be true. Having a belief does not necessarily mean something is fact. It only means that in your mind it is fact. Several hundred years ago, in the minds of many, the thought *the Earth is flat* was believed to be fact.

Of the thousands of beliefs that reside deep within your subconscious, some of them are about you and who you are as a person. They describe whether you are *smart* or *dumb*, *attractive* or *ugly*, *successful* or a *failure*. All these beliefs are thoughts you think to be true about yourself.

You are probably thinking *what does that have to do with anything?* Well, your subconscious is powerful, so powerful in fact that it takes your internally held beliefs and connects to your intellect, body, and emotions to make you the person you believe yourself to be. That means, if over the years you have accepted limiting beliefs such as *success is difficult to achieve*, *it is hard to be creative*, or *math is*

21

impossible, your subconscious is doing everything in its power to make your behaviors consistent with these beliefs.

It is causing you to make more than the normal amount of mistakes in your work. It is preventing you from performing at your peak level. It is influencing how you perceive risks. More importantly, it is intimidating you into letting opportunity after opportunity pass you by. Regardless of your true mental or physical capacity, if the limiting belief is fact in your mind, it is fact in your life and you won't be able to see or do things any other way!

On the other hand, if you have positive, encouraging beliefs, beliefs that are open to the possibilities, your subconscious will allow you to feel powerful, capable, and in control. It will support you when you go for that promotion, work toward your goals, and live the life others dream about. With a mindset of positive, reassuring beliefs, failure is not an option.

Your subconscious beliefs influence more than just your abilities. The world within your subconscious can even change the physical structure of your body and create a world with or without health. That is to say, maintaining health has more to it than taking a pill or watching what you eat. Health is a state of mind, and the power of the subconscious can be greater than anything a doctor has to offer.

Many examples confirm this idea, but none better than the placebo effect. Placebos are pills that consist of nothing more than sugar and distilled water. More and more, doctors are discovering that many illnesses may be cured just by giving patients placebos and convincing them the placebos are actual medicine. Since no real medication is given to these patients, the placebo effect proves that a state of mind alone can affect a person's health.

Placebo effects go beyond taking pills. Surgery proves its impact as well. Between 1995 and 1998, surgeon J. Bruce Moseley conducted an experiment with 180 patients, all suffering from arthritic pain in their knees. While 59 patients received the standard procedure, scraping and rinsing of the knee joint, 61 received only the rinsing, and the remaining 60 received no surgery at all. Doctors put every patient on crutches, sent them home, and documented their progress over a 24-month period. Everyone in the study reported feeling substantially better and happy with the outcome, even the ones who did not receive surgery.[1] Because all believed they received actual surgery, their bodies responded and their condition improved.

---

[1] The New England Journal of Medicine (A Controlled Trial of Arthroscopic Surgery for Osteoarthritis of the Knee July 11, 2002 347: 81-88.)

The state of mind that placebos put a person in is so remarkable that the government requires all medicine to be tested against a placebo before it is released to the public. Furthermore, many treatments have been taken off the shelf when research determined that healing occurred solely due to the placebo effect. In the case of the pharmaceutical giant Merck, its proposed anti-depressant MK-869 never even made it to the shelves because the placebo prescription proved to be equally effective in improving the patients' health.

The opposite can also be true. People can develop and exhibit symptoms of diseases simply through believing strongly enough that something is wrong with them. Leading medical research says that as much as 75% of sicknesses in people arise from some sort of hypochondria or imaginary illness. These people do not have an actual disorder that makes them sick. Their disorder comes from their belief that they are sick or likely to become sick. It's as if the subconscious takes their belief and produces the symptoms of the sickness they think they have. This is the power of beliefs to affect your health.

There are many more examples of how the subconscious uses your inner beliefs to influence your mind and body. One such example includes phantom pregnancies, or *pseudocyesis*, where a woman will show signs of pregnancy—milk production, expanded stomach, lack of period—if she believes strongly enough that she is in fact pregnant, even though she is not. This is another case that illustrates the effects of beliefs.

The intention is not to claim that all limitations and ill health are a result of negative beliefs. Though, it is quite remarkable just how much subconsciously held beliefs—whether they are rooted in fact or not—influence your physical and mental well-being, as well as your ability to perform.

Therefore, if you want to perform better, become healthier, feel happier, or improve the quality of your life in any way, shape or form, it helps to start by replacing limiting and self-defeating beliefs within your subconscious. It isn't enough to alter what comes into your conscious; you also have to replace what already exists in your subconscious. By changing your unconscious beliefs about who you are and what you are capable of, you set in motion the process necessary to manifest the changes you desire.

Going back to the point we made earlier, you can change your inner beliefs by changing your self-talk. The principle of the mind says that your thoughts guide the function of your subconscious mind. You can use this principle to concentrate your self-talk to redirect your unconscious. By doing this, you create beliefs that make your mind work for you instead of against you.

How to Use Self-talk to Change Your Beliefs from the Negative to Positive

Before you can change your subconscious beliefs, you need to take stock of what they are. To do this, take a minute and think about the many self-defeating beliefs that run your life, those that come up in your mind on an ongoing basis. They constantly remind you that you are not good enough, smart enough, or up to the mark in some way. The statements go something like *I'm a moron*, *No one likes me*, *I can't do anything right*, *Success is just too hard*.

Take 8-12 of these negative beliefs, the ones that connect with you at a core level, and write them in the column labeled Self-Defeating Beliefs below. Carefully observe the negative quality of these statements and opinions. Even though they feel real to you, and even though you can't imagine yourself without them, realize that these beliefs are *not* who you are. They don't own you, and neither do you own them, so it's OK to free yourself from the havoc they create.

Self-Defeating Beliefs	Self-Supporting Beliefs
1.	1.
2.	2.
3.	3.
4.	4.
5.	5.
6.	6.
7.	7.
8.	8.
9.	9.
10.	10.

In order to liberate yourself from their effects, think of 8-12 positive beliefs that counter these defeating beliefs. Focus not just on neutralizing the negative beliefs, but also on the type of person you want to become. Write them in the column labeled Self-Supporting Beliefs. Some examples could be *I am smart*, *I am healthy*, *I am organized,* and *I do things right*.

Now close your eyes, take a deep breath, relax, and repeat each self-supporting belief to yourself 10 times. Do this on a daily basis until they start to reverse your old way of being.

The above is a great exercise to rid yourself of negative beliefs that hold you back and keep you down. Remember, negative beliefs not only distort reality, but they prevent you from achieving your goals, and they trigger emotions that immobilize and distress you. What's more, they make you feel powerless, and few things in life are more debilitating than believing you have no power, no ability to control the things that happen to you, and no way to choose the life you want to lead. You end up feeling like a victim at the mercy of forces beyond your control. As a result, you never feel fulfilled.

With the above exercise, you can stop this vicious cycle. People have been able to make miraculous changes by changing their core beliefs using self-talk in this way. It is the equivalent of installing anti-virus software that goes in and destroys negative programming within your mind. Just as with any computer, when you remove the harmful viruses, you run smoother, faster, and more efficiently.

Support Behavior or Habit Change

Another way to apply self-talk is to support a change in behavior or habit. You can use self-talk to help you stop a habit—like smoking. You can use it to help you start a routine—like exercising, or you can use it to help you improve something that you already do—like your memory or a golf swing.

Self-talk supports behavior change on two levels. First, when you repeat statements that you are a person of a specific behavior or habit, you create beliefs that you are this type of person. As you learned, your actions more naturally follow the path of your internally held beliefs.

Conversely, when you try to change without first changing your beliefs, the process tends to be more challenging. Take smoking, for example. If you are a smoker and believe that you can't quit, your mind will override any of your efforts to quit because it has difficulty acting outside of its internally held beliefs. It sees you as a smoker who can't quit, and that's what it acts out. Self-talk works because it helps you change that belief from the negative to the positive.

Second, as you learned earlier, your thoughts, in many ways, guide your decisions and actions. When you repeat a self-talk statement, you guide your actions in that direction. Thus, if you affirm that you do a particular behavior or act in a certain manner, you will more easily perform that behavior or act out in that manner.

Let's look at another example. Say you want to learn to play basketball, but the self-talk running through your head is *I can't dribble* or *I am a poor shooter*. When you start playing, what's more likely to happen—you dribbling/shooting well or poorly? More than likely, you're going to start off poorly. You are going to slip up in ways that reinforce the above self-talk statements. Even worse, you're probably going to progress slowly as well.

On the other hand, if you use self-talk to affirm that *I dribble the ball well, I am a good shooter*, and *I make my shots*, that will help you develop better dribbling and shooting habits and help you progress much quicker. It will do that because your thoughts support your actions, as your mind and body respond to your thinking.

So now that you know how self-talk can help you in this area, let's go more in detail with the specific techniques.

How to Use Self-talk to Change Behaviors and Habits

To use self-talk for behavior and habit change, pick an area you want to change or improve; then create 10-12 self-talk statements that cover the change you want in that area. When creating the statements, address not only the progress you desire, but also the issues you might have to confront (this can include fears you have to overcome).

Taking the example of smoking again, you would start by writing down, *I am a non-smoker, I quit this habit from my life*. Then you would follow it up with certain issues you might face in your efforts to quit. For example, if you have a hard time saying no to people when they offer you cigarettes, you can manage this issue by including into the mix a self-talk affirmation like *I easily say no when someone offers me a cigarette*. You want to make sure that you hit on every facet of the goal and problem with precise and complete instructions.

We can try to explain each and every aspect of this, but it will be much easier to show you. In the following pages are examples of how a set of self-talk statements might look for each type of change—stop habit, start habit, and improve performance—you might choose to create.

STOP HABIT – SMOKING

I can quit smoking. Being a non-smoker is easy for me. I naturally overcome any habits I choose.

I reject the idea that smoking is attractive and I eliminate it from my life.

I was born as a non-smoker and I choose to live my life as a non-smoker. I see myself as walking, talking, and thinking like a non-smoker.

I take good care of my mind and body. My lungs are strong and healthy. I breathe in only clean, clear air.

When I see a cigarette, I mentally say, 'I am free from this habit,' and I am. If someone offers me a cigarette, I easily say no.

START HABIT - EXERCISE

I exercise on a regular basis. Exercising is fun. I enjoy exercising regularly.

As I exercise I can feel the fat inside me melting. I can feel my muscles becoming taut and strong.

Each day, in every way I am getting stronger and healthier. I feel the rush of strength into my body. Already, I feel more in shape.

I keep myself fit. I eat and drink only what keeps me whole. I believe in my ability to maintain healthy habits.

My body is precious. I am taking good care of it by eating and drinking foods that help it grow.

IMPROVE PERFORMANCE - MEMORY

I have an excellent memory.

My subconscious is an information warehouse. It records everything I see, hear and do.

I easily remember dates, names, facts, formulas, directions or anything else I choose.

I can easily recall where I put things. I recall information effortlessly. I can recall information that is important to me.

My memory is well organized. My brain files information for easy retrieval. I have excellent concentration.

I am happy and proud of my ability to remember. I have a strong memory and it gets better every day.

Notice how each set of statements gets specific and paints a complete picture of the results you want. It includes statements of your end goal while adding dialogue to help you neutralize specific challenges you might encounter. You can put together these types of focused self-talk affirmations for all types of situations and circumstances, whether you want to be a better test taker and tennis player or whether you want to increase your confidence and lower your anxiety. All you need to do is write a set of self-talk statements that affirm the qualities you want in an area and then repeat them daily.

This technique has great power in manifesting change. It not only helps you reprogram, but also helps you change your beliefs from *no I can't* to *yes I can*. As mentioned several times, changing your beliefs is vital to any success. By getting your subconscious to believe that you can quit smoking or that you can start exercising, you allow yourself to move more easily in these directions. Once your subconscious mind begins to accept your new directives (*I am a non-smoker* or *I am healthy and strong*), it is only a matter of time before projected changes become reality.

Shift Focus and Energy, in the moment, from the Negative to the Positive

So far you have learned to use self-talk to overcome negative beliefs picked up from your past. You have also learned how to use self-talk to support behavioral change which reshapes your future. Next, you will learn how to use self-talk to shift your focus and energy during times of streaming negativity to maintain composure in the present.

Judi Brown King, an Olympic silver medalist in the 400-meter hurdles, describes how she uses self-talk in the moment to maintain composure during a race. She says:

> ...instead of thinking, "I'm tired," or possibly, "I'm behind," I concentrate on staying relaxed by saying, "Stay relaxed." If I hit a hurdle, I say "It's okay...let's make up the momentum you have lost." I tell myself "Okay, you're still in good shape, up with the top three runners, let's try to get up in second or first so there are no more mishaps." Things like that. I give myself continuous pep talks.

Like Judi Brown King, you can give yourself this kind of pep talk to shift your focus from the negative to the positive. For example, if you start to get anxious about your 2 o'clock presentation, instead of mouthing off how nervous you are, change your self-talk to *I am confident and in control.* It may not completely change your circumstance, but it will help you remain calm so you can maintain your energy to better deal with the situation.

Or if you feel overwhelmed by a task ahead of you, and for whatever reason you fear that you will miss the deadline, you can switch your negative state of mind by changing your inner dialogue. Tell yourself, *I can do it, I am a do-it-now person, I do things now*. Again, this will not make the assignment go away, but the statement will connect to you internally and trigger a response that will help you get it done in a timely manner.

In a slightly different scenario, say you encounter an inevitable bad moment that just plain ruins your day. Some road-raged driver cuts in front of you in traffic and needlessly flips you off, or your in-the-moment irrational spouse picks a fight with you early in the morning about something extraneous. These events have a tendency to blow out of proportion and downright spoil your day. It's as if the incident ignites a fuse, and it's just a matter of time before it reaches a barrel full of explosives to cause an enormous blast.

Rather than letting these events spoil your day, you can use self-talk to keep your cool and eliminate any self-induced stress. You can tell yourself *it's not the end of the world* or *I will not let this incident affect my day* (saying the statements calmly and matter of fact, not forcing it). You might follow these statements with *I am calm and I feel relaxed*. By doing this, you interrupt the pattern of thought before it escalates into something destructive, like killing the fuse trail before it reaches the barrel.

Lastly, it's important to note that sometimes negative thoughts and emotions surface without any sort of triggers. There is no presentation, assignment, or bad moment to cause you to feel down. You may not be able to figure out why, but the feelings are there. Usually, this is out of habit. Your mind and body have become so accustomed to certain thoughts or emotions, that they become a part of you. Again, in these instances, you can counter their presence with positive self-talk.

This is the kind of conscious pep talk you can apply with difficult "in the moment" situations. Whether you feel overwhelmed by the tasks ahead of you or bogged down by a series of misfortunes in your life, the conscious use of concentrated self-talk will help you retain your perspective in the present.

There you have it. These are the three ways to apply self-talk—replace limiting beliefs, support a change in behavior or habit, and change your mood in the moment. While most human beings lose their grip when the going gets tough, winners get sharper and more focused. It is their ability to bend thoughts to their will that makes these people different from the millions struggling behind. Self-talk gives you the power to bend thoughts to your will.

CHAPTER 3 - HOW TO WORD YOUR SELF-TALK

If you hear a voice within you saying, "You are not a painter," then by all means paint and that voice will be silenced.—Vincent Van Gogh

With the many examples of self-talk given above, you can probably recognize a good self-talk affirmation when you read one. The words empower you and create a magical shift in feeling. Still, could you explain what exactly makes a self-talk statement create that empowering shift?

Effective self-talk affirmations are not offhand sentences that you mouth off randomly. They are structured to focus on the end result and help you deal directly with issues and problems which frustrate and hold you back.

To achieve this, effective self-talk statements should be:

• Short and Concise

• Positively Worded

• Phrased in the Present Tense

Short and Concise

Read the following self-talk statement out loud to yourself:

> *Whenever I set an explicit goal, I take instantaneous action toward its fulfillment by developing and maintaining tremendous energy. I put myself in a high state of total certainty, believing full well that I can create any positive situation that I put my mind to.*

Did any part of that statement really stick in your mind? Probably not. The above statements are lengthy, confusing and complicated. Making the statements confusing and complicated sends a message to your subconscious that you want things to be complicated.

Instead, make your self-talk statement brief and simple. A much better alternative is to break down the statement into several shorter, more concise phrases:

> *I enjoy setting goals. Goals are fun and easy to achieve. I am committed to accomplishing my goal of losing 20 lbs.*

Read these statements aloud and feel the difference between the two versions.

Positive

Make your self-talk as positive as possible, always affirming what you want rather than telling yourself what you don't want. For example, *I am not stressed out* is a negative statement. Your mind is a visual machine, and thinking about stress is easier for it than not thinking about stress.

To illustrate, if someone tells you, *don't think of a black cat*, what is the first thing that pops into your mind? Exactly, a black cat. Your mind doesn't hear the words *no*, *not*, and *don't*. So when you say, *I'm not stressed out*, the image your mind automatically creates is of *stress*.

A better alternative to use is *I am calm in body and mind*. Can you feel the difference when you say *I am calm in body and mind* versus *I am not stressed out*? The former evokes an image of peace and serenity, making it easier to achieve a relaxed, stress-free state.

Present Tense

How many times have you told yourself you will do something? How many times did you get it done? You probably tell yourself over and over that you will lose weight, find a new job, or that you will be more successful, but has that proven effective? Probably not.

When you say you *will* or you are *going to* do something, your mind hears it as later, not today. Someday *I will be rich*, *I will be a non-smoker*, or *I am going to be slim and healthy*, but, as for the present, there is no need for change. The results you want will always be waiting to happen. Eventually, the present becomes the future, and the future never arrives.

If you want to create change, your inner attention must be focused on the change you desire. For this reason, affirm all of your self-talk statements in the present tense, as if the desired change has already taken place. Say *I am successful* rather than *I will be successful*. That way, your subconscious mind starts to make this work now.

In the beginning, it may be difficult for you to accept some presently worded self-talk. That is, if you are overweight, repeating *I am my ideal weight* might be too hard for your subconscious to believe. In these instances, you can rephrase the statement to focus on a process rather than an end result. Instead of saying *I am my ideal weight*, try *each day I get closer to my ideal weight*, or *I have total confidence I will reach my ideal weight*.

Changing the statement in this way eliminates unnecessary resistance, yet the words still move you in the right direction—as the example used here, towards losing weight. As you gain confidence and begin to accept your self-talk more easily, you can change the wording of the statement to be more precise, like *I am my ideal weight*.

You now have all the required elements to word your self-talk statements effectively—short and concise, positive, and present tense. It is important that you incorporate these elements into your self-talk affirmations as best you can. They will make your thoughts more permeable, allowing you to manifest the results you want quicker.

Now that you know how to word your self-talk, in the next chapter, we will discuss how to verbalize these statements.

CHAPTER 4 – HOW TO VERBALIZE YOUR SELF-TALK

I talk to myself because I like dealing with a better class of people. —Savielly Tartakower

So far you have learned how changing your self-talk can improve the quality of your life. In addition, you have learned how to word your self-talk for maximum effectiveness. These things alone, however, are not going to make your self-talk a state of mind.

For your self-talk to resonate at a core level, you must express it:

• With Belief

• With Emotion

• In a relaxed state, and

• Repeated often.

Doing so gives your message authority and power in your subconscious. These are the glue that makes the thought stick in your mind.

Belief

When you tell yourself that you are smart, capable, and energetic, say it as if there is no way you could be anything else. Believe in it as strongly as you believe that the Earth is round or the sky is blue. Whatever you believe strongly in, no matter how farfetched, will ultimately become your reality.

If you repeat *I am smart*, but in the back of your mind you have doubt, you weaken the process. Forget your current circumstances for the moment and focus on a different reality, your ideal reality. Gandhi made this point when he said: *The man I want to become, if I believe myself to be, I will become.*

Belief also means letting go of any feelings of wanting. Want creates lack. When you want something, within you a feeling of lack is created because you don't have it. When you repeat statements of change, but deep down all you feel is *wanting* the change, then you are not in belief, and the affirmations won't be as effective. Therefore, say these statements as if you already have the changes you desire. Your affirmation does not have to be shouted or defended—it simply is. Truly successful people do not need to prove themselves to anybody because they already know success is their reality.

Emotion

There are two languages of the subconscious mind. Your subconscious communicates in pictures and emotions. Emotions play an important part in our lives. They push us into action or keep us from acting. Some people say that unless you make a person feel something, he or she will not hear you. The same goes for your subconscious.

Even more important, our memories are linked to emotions. Meaning, we tend to remember things that have a strong emotional relevance to us. If you think back to a fearful or triumphant moment, you'll realize that you remember it in painstaking detail. You can recollect the exact day and time of the event, where you were and who you were with, and so on.

If you want your subconscious to take note of what you are saying, then, you need to affirm your statements with positive emotions. When you say *I am smart and capable*, don't say it in a dull manner, as though you are reading the newspaper. Say it with enthusiasm. Be passionate and involve your emotions. Every time you fulfill a need, a positive feeling arises. Simply evoke that positive feeling when you engage yourself in the affirmation. Positive emotions bring the messages to life.

Relaxed State

It is important to be relaxed when you repeat your self-talk statements. The subconscious is more active when you are less active. As a result, it is able to receive and store more information. In addition, in a relaxed state, there is less distraction between the conscious and subconscious, so there is less resistance to the statements.

To get into a relaxed state, do the following. Take in a slow deep breath. Hold it for five seconds, and then slowly exhale as you mentally say *relax*. Take another slow, deep breath. Hold it for another five to ten seconds. Again, slowly exhale as you say *relax*. Continue this rhythmic mantra for one to two minutes.

Now get into a comfortable position. Close your eyes and release any mental stress. Feel your shoulders relax and your jaw unclench. Feel yourself sink into whatever you are sitting or lying on. No muscles are flexed.

Notice how you feel calm, slowed down, less tense, and more open to suggestions and instructions. As you unwind in this feeling, take a set of self-talk affirmations you worked on earlier and repeat each one 10 times. Start by repeating the first statement you wrote. Next, move to the second one, then to the third and on and on until you affirm all 10 – 12 items on the list. After you finish, slowly open your eyes and come back to the present awareness. Tell yourself with utmost confidence that you have all that you just affirmed.

Obviously, if you are using self-talk as an in-the-moment tool to change the direction of your energy and emotion, you do not have to do this relaxation exercise. When you are doing a set of self-talk statements to change your beliefs or habits, however, it is highly recommended that you move yourself into a calm state before you repeat the affirmations.

Repetition

In order to entrench positive and enriching thoughts in your mind, you must repeat your self-talk statements often. A lifetime of crusty and restricting beliefs cannot be set right through wishful thinking. If it were that easy, you could become Abe Lincoln one day and Roosevelt the next.

Your current mindset is a result of repetitive messages, and it will take some repetition for your subconscious to turn that around. That means you have to follow a strict routine of repetition to challenge and change your beliefs. An effective routine is to affirm a set of self-talk statements twice a day (preferably once at night just before bed and once in the morning before starting off your day) for at least 30 days. Consistency is key. If you do this regularly, your brain will get accustomed to what it's hearing from you until it's convinced that you're virtually destined to turn your words into reality.

49

These are the guidelines for verbalizing your self-talk—affirm with belief, use emotions, get into a relaxed state, and repeat the statements often. They are the necessary ingredients that turn your self-talk from mere words to a powerful agent for self-growth, development, and improvement. Take these to heart so you can easily and effortlessly self-talk your way to success.

CONCLUSION

It's not who you are that holds you back, it's who you think you're not.—Author Unknown

In the beginning, saying positive things to yourself may feel weird. You may feel silly, like *Saturday Night Live's* character Stuart Smalley and his infamous quote *...because I'm good enough, I'm smart enough, and doggonit, people like me!* It may seem that what you are affirming is not true. You may even feel that you are lying to yourself. When you say *I am smart and talented*, your inner voice may react with, *are you kidding*?

If you put in the energy and dedicate yourself to talking positively to yourself, though, you will begin to believe that you are smart, capable, successful, healthy, and worthy of it. The subconscious mind does not argue—it simply performs. Once you accept that something is true, your subconscious works to make it true. If you tell your subconscious over and over that you are capable and successful, it will accept it as such and bring results.

If you do nothing else, then, begin talking positive to yourself. Whether you take nothing away from this book or take everything, talk in a way that is constructive and supportive. Learn to pay attention to your thoughts. If they sound negative, reverse them right away. *I'm an idiot* turns into *I am smart and capable, I do things right.*

Self-talk is a two-way street. It can build or destroy. The way you use it decides the results you are going to have.

Who you are is not who you were, and it doesn't mean it's who you have to be – Kamran Akhter

* * *

From reading this book, you can see self-talk is not a difficult technique. It requires little in terms of time, energy, and effort. You need only create a set of statements that describe the changes you desire, and then repeat those statements daily.

Due to its straight forward nature, this book was kept concise as possible. If you notice, it's free from filler or unnecessary language and discusses only the essential points for using and succeeding with the technique. This way you are not wasting time reading about what to do, but instead, you can start with the material right away.

More importantly, I believe that for a development tool to be effective, it must be simple to learn, understand, and use. I'm sure you've come across fantastic tools in 200+ page books, but never got around to putting them to use. The mere fact that it took 200 pages to explain the concepts means they were too complicated to begin with. With this book, the goal was to give you something that was simple, yet effective, while keeping it simple.

With that said, I hope you found the explanation useful, informative, and easy to grasp. If you did, I would appreciate it if you could leave a positive review of this book on Amazon or where you made the purchase. It will motivate others to learn more about self-talk and its benefits.

To ensure you put self-talk into practice, I recommend getting the audio edition of this book. Even though what's presented here is simple and straightforward, you'd be surprised just how easily you can forget it. That's because your old habits and routines would much rather have you avoid doing or remembering anything that can move your life in a different direction, even if it is a better direction. So it's important to review the information regularly. With the audio, it's easy to regularly review the material as you can play it in the background or listen to it passively while doing other tasks. This way the techniques always stay on top of mind, instead of getting drowned in the course of your daily life.

Also, this book has over 20 self-talk scripts in the following pages of the appendix. The audio edition narrates all of these scripts in a relaxing, soothing tone. You can pick a self-talk script for an area you desire and follow along and repeat the statements as the narrator recites them, making it not only easier to affirm, but creating more weight in your unconscious. You can find out how to get your free audio copy at www.bitly.com/selfaudio

Self-talk goes hand in hand with two other very important concepts: Goal Setting and Visualization. If you really want to enhance your abilities and success, consider also reading:

Goal Setting: Discover What You Want in Life and Achieve it Faster than You Think Possible by Kamran Akhter

The Art & Science of Visualization: A Practical Guide for Self-Help, Self-Healing, and Improving Other Areas of Yourself by Kamran Akhter

APPENDIX – SELF-TALK STATEMENTS FOR LIFE'S MANY STRUGGLES

As simple as self-talk is, it can take time and effort to put together the right set of statements, especially ones that hone in on and resonate with the specific changes you desire. To prevent this obstacle from getting in the way of you starting, the following pages provide pre-defined sets of self-talk statements for the many goals, issues, and challenges you may want to achieve, improve, or overcome. They cover everything from having more money, success, and motivation to enjoying better health, love, and happiness.

To get started, pick statements from one or two of these areas and repeat each statement 10 times, twice daily. If you pick two areas to work on, affirm statements from one area in the morning and the other area in the evening. For example, if you want to work on happiness and confidence, repeat the set of statements for happiness in the morning and then the set for confidence in the evening. If you choose to focus only on one area, say confidence, then repeat statements for confidence both in the morning and evening.

Whatever you do, focus on only one or two sets of statements at a time. You don't want to overexert yourself with three, four, five or more sets of statements at once. It's just too much for your mind. Also, spend at least 30 to 90 days on each set. Otherwise you may not see the results you desire.

If there isn't a specific issue or sticking point that stands out for your, feel free to combine statements from different areas to form your own set. Also, feel free to add in your own statements or change any statements to fit your needs. Either way, make sure to keep your sets between 8 - 12 statements, but no more than 15.

Again, if you prefer to affirm the statements by following along on audio, you can get your audio copy at www.bitly.com/selfaudio

Self-Talk for Happiness:

- I am happy.

- I choose to be happy in the here and now.

- There is no limit to how happy I can feel.

- My life is filled with pleasure and joy.

- I accept all that is good and beautiful in my life.

- I deserve to laugh and have fun.

- I laugh and play like a child.

- I appreciate the present moment.

- I have everything I need, and nothing I don't.

- I'm content with my place in this world.

- I release all experiences of unhappiness.

- I'm happy when others succeed.

- I remove jealousy from my life.

- I enjoy life's simple pleasures.

- Life is wonderful.

Self-Talk for Confidence:

- I am strong and confident.

- I believe in myself.

- I believe in who I am and where I am going.

- I have confidence in my skills and abilities.

- I have the ability to grow and develop.

- I am self-assured.

- I am capable.

- I am proud.

- I trust myself.

- I trust myself to make the right decisions and choices.

- I act in spite of fear.

- I am talented, creative, and successful.

- My potential is unlimited.

- Each day, in every way I am becoming more self-assured.

- I stand unshaken in any situation I encounter.

Self-Talk for Positive Thinking:

- I am positive and optimistic.

- I find it easy to think and be optimistic.

- I focus only on the positive in my life.

- I find it easy to stay positive.

- I look on bright side of everything.

- I enthusiastically look forward to each new day.

- My life is going smooth.

- Everything goes my way.

- Fantastic opportunities await me in all areas of my life.

- I let go of dwelling on negative outcomes.

- I believe things will always work out for me.

- Everything is working out for my best interest.

- Life is rewarding and fun.

- I'm remain optimistic, no matter what.

- All that I need comes to me at the right time.

Self-Talk for Taking Action and Productivity:

- I am a do it now person.

- I do things now.

- I accomplish everything right away.

- I complete tasks, goals, and projects quickly, easily, and effortlessly.

- I find it easy to start tasks.

- I always finish any task that I start.

- I make things happen now.

- I take action in the moment.

- I am organized, efficient, and productive.

- It is normal to start projects early.

- Taking immediate action is a natural part of what I do.

- I enjoy finishing difficult tasks.

- I know exactly what needs to be done and I do it.

- I am accomplished and proud.

- I take charge and act now.

Self-Talk for Self-Esteem:

• I like myself. I like who I am and where I am going.

• I deserve, have permission, and can have good things in my life.

• I do my very best every day and that's enough.

• I accept myself completely and love myself deeply

• I cherish my imperfections.

• I am unique and I love it.

• I deserve health, wealth, and success.

• I am worthy of love, joy, and happiness.

• I am o.k. with who I am.

• I respect myself at all times

• I change what I can and accept what I cannot.

• What I cannot change, I embrace.

• I let go of thinking that I haven't been good enough.

• I trust my creative gifts

• I am a beautiful person inside and out

Self-Talk for Concentration:

• I have strong power of concentration.

• I am focused.

• I easily focus on any task or activity I choose.

• My mind is alert and attentive.

• My mind stays on tasks and activities without wandering.

• I pay attention. It is easy for me to pay attention. I enjoy paying attention.

• I calmly focus my full attention on tasks at hand.

• My thoughts are controlled and organized.

• I am free from mental clutter and distractions.

• I naturally ignore distractions.

• I can concentrate on any chore, assignment, errand, goal, or project with ease.

• My mind is aware and observant at all times. It pays attention to what it reads, hears, and sees.

• I hear everything that is said in conversations with others.

• I register every sentence of any material I read.

• I pick up on everything that I watch or see.

Self-Talk for Assertiveness:

• I am a calm, confident communicator.

• I stand up for my rights.

• I easily ask for what I want and effortlessly exercise my right to say no.

• I do not feel bad for asking what I want or need.

• I naturally express my thoughts, opinions, and desires.

• I express my thoughts and opinions with confidence.

• I am unselfconscious and I am unconcerned with what others think.

• I am in control. I don't let people and outside influences destabilize me.

• I easily express myself to others without fear.

• I speak my mind without hesitation.

• I stand up for myself and my beliefs.

• I don't control others or allow others to control me.

• I say no whenever I choose.

• I am becoming more and more assertive each day.

• I can assert myself in any situation.

Self-Talk for Attracting Money:

• Money is flowing to me in avalanches of abundance.

• Money pours into my life easily, frequently, and abundantly.

• I am a money magnet, I attract money naturally.

• I am attracting more and more money every day.

• I release all my negative beliefs about money and invite wealth into my life

• I am creating wealth and financial stability.

• I deserve wealth and financial stability.

• I have the ability to make large sums of money.

• It comes to me from many sources continually.

• Money is everywhere, all I need is to grab it.

• I am making money doing what I love.

• I have all the money I need.

• Financial success and abundance are mine.

• There are many ways to make money, and I always find a way.

• I enjoy a lifestyle of luxury.

Self-Talk for Managing Money:

• I am responsible with money.

• I save money.

• I find it easy to save money.

• Saving money feels good.

• I spend money wisely.

• I have a tight control on my expenses.

• My expenses never exceed my income.

• I always make sensible and informed spending decisions.

• I resist temptations to spend money.

• It feels good when I resist the temptation to spend.

• I am highly disciplined and never feel pressure to spend money.

• I have complete control of my money.

• I am in control of my finances.

• I handle my finances with care and attention.

• I have complete awareness of how I'm spend, save, and invest money.

Self-Talk for Health:

• I am healthy and strong

• I am filled with energy, vitality, and beauty.

• I deserve health. It is my right to be healthy. I give myself permission to have good health.

• My immune system is strong and powerful. It protects and heals me.

• I do not fear illness because my immune system always restores me to my best.

• I love and care for my body and it cares for me.

• I abandon unhealthy habits and take up new, beneficial ones.

• I give my mind and body the nourishing, revitalizing rest it needs.

• Any sickness or disease I have is being cured.

• I am healing. My body is healing. My mind is healing.

• I heal quickly.

• Every day in every way, I'm getting better, better, and better.

• Diet and exercise is the golden road to good health.

• I exercise and eat healthy. I enjoy exercising and eating healthy.

• I am free of ill health.

Self-Talk for Anxiety:

- I am calm and relaxed

- I am at peace.

- I am safe.

- I feel safe and protected.

- I am cool, calm, and collected.

- With every breath, I get more and more calm.

- I release all fears.

- I release, let go, and relax.

- Every cell in my body is relaxed

- I am o.k. with where I am right now.

- I remain calm, regardless of the situation.

- All tension is gone from my mind and body.

- I'm free from all symptoms of stress and anxiety.

- I'm free of all fear about the future.

- Peace of mind and I are one.

Self-Talk for Panic Attacks:

- I'm going to be all right.

- I accept what I am feeling.

- This feeling cannot hurt me.

- The feeling is irrational. It does not mean anything bad will happen.

- There is no real cause for this panic.

- I'm safe and protected

- I choose to accept panic and not run from it.

- I remain calm regardless of what's going on with my emotions.

- I can feel panic and still focus on the task at hand.

- I feel the fear and do it anyways.

- This feeling will leave all by itself. I do not have to do anything.

- Panic is a lie, there is nothing wrong.

- I am proud of myself.

- I am no longer afraid.

- I'm free from all of the physical effects of panic and anxiety.

Self-Talk for Depression:

- I am free from depression.

- I overcome this emotional limitation. It is easy for me to overcome limitations.

- I am overcoming my mental state to be more joyous & happy.

- My mood is improving each day.

- I feel energetic and alive. I am full of energy and vitality.

- I feel good. I feel great. I feel in control.

- I am gaining more control of my thoughts, feelings, and emotions.

- I find joy in simple pleasures.

- I concentrate on activities that make me feel good.

- I accept the pain and discomfort in my life. Only when I accept pain, can I transcend it.

- I am a silent warrior.

- I forgive myself completely. I forgive everyone who has ever been unkind to me.

- I let go of shame, guilt, and embarrassment.

- I release all anger, anxiety, disappointment, fear, resentment, and worry.

- I am positive, hopeful, and optimistic.

Self-Talk for Alcohol Addiction:

• I am alcohol free.

• My mental and physical addictions are behind me now.

• I am sober. I enjoy being sober. I have fun when I am sober.

• It's o.k. to be sober when others are not.

• I am in control of my thoughts, emotions, decisions, & actions.

• I am a strong, in control person with healthy habits.

• I magically release that which I no longer need or want in life

• I refrain from alcohol easily, naturally, and effortlessly.

• I triumph over peer pressure. No one has power to influence my decisions and actions.

• I can say no to others. I say no to others. When someone offers me a drink, I easily say "no!"

• I refuse alcohol. I find it easy to refuse alcohol. I am not tempted by drinking one bit.

• I let go of unhealthy relationships & remove negative influence from my life. I have no loyalty or obligation to such people.

• I attract only positive, healthy, supportive people into my life.

• When I am bored, I resort to constructive activities to fill time.

• When I feel nervous or uneasy, I deal with it in healthy ways – by taking a break, a nap, a bath, or watching a funny movie.

Self-Talk for Drug Addiction:

• I am drug and addiction free.

• My mental and physical addictions are behind me now.

• I am sober. I enjoy being sober. I have fun when I am sober.

• It's o.k. to be sober when others are not.

• I am in control of my thoughts, emotions, decisions, & actions.

• I am a strong, in control person with healthy habits.

• I magically release that which I no longer need or want in life.

• I refrain from substances easily, naturally, and effortlessly.

• I triumph over peer pressure. No one has power to influence my decisions and actions.

• I can say no to others. I say no to others. When someone offers me drugs, I easily say "no!"

• I refuse drugs. I find it easy to refuse drugs. I am not tempted by drugs one bit.

• I let go of unhealthy relationships & remove negative influence from my life. I have no loyalty or obligation to such people.

• I attract only positive, healthy, supportive people into my life.

• When I am bored, I resort to constructive activities to fill time.

• When I feel nervous or uneasy, I deal with it in healthy ways – I take a break, a nap, a bath, or watch a funny movie.

Self-Talk for Healthy Body Image:

• I like my body.

• I like how it looks and how it feels

• I am comfortable in my body.

• I accept my body fully, deeply, and joyfully.

• My body has its own wisdom, and I trust its wisdom completely.

• My body is a projection of my beliefs about myself.

• My beliefs are growing more beautiful and luminous every day.

• I see the divine perfection in each and every one of my cells.

• I welcome my scars, wrinkles, folds, and everything else.

• Flaws are transformed by my acceptance.

• As I love myself, I allow others to love me too.

• Today I choose to honor my beauty, my strength, and my uniqueness.

• I love the way I feel when I take good care of myself.

• Today, my well-being is top priority.

• My body is not perfect, but that is o.k. No body is perfect

Self-Talk for Success:

• I am successful.

• I succeed in everything I do.

• I am a cause in the world.

• Failure is only a feeling. It will not hold me back.

• Today I am willing to fail in order to succeed.

• I can master anything if I do it enough times.

• I have the strength to make my dreams come true.

• I'm going to relax and have fun with this, no matter what the outcome may be.

• I'm proud of myself for trying. Most people won't even do that.

• I put my full trust in my inner intelligence.

• I grow in strength with every step I take.

• I move past hesitation and make room for victory.

• With a solid plan and a belief in myself, there's nothing I can't do.

• I have all of the talent, skill, and motivation to accomplish all that I desire.

• I visualize success and then make it happen

Self-Talk for Abundance and Prosperity:

• I live a life of abundance.

• I am open to the door of abundance in all areas of my life.

• I now have everything I need.

• Thank you, thank you, thank you, and thank you.

• I am expanding my awareness of the abundance all around me.

• I allow the universe to bring me abundance in surprising and joyful ways.

• My heart is a magnet that attracts more of everything I desire.

• Prosperity surrounds me, prosperity fills me, and prosperity flows to me and through me.

• I exude passion, purpose, and prosperity.

• I am always led to the people who need what I have to offer and offer what I need.

• As my commitment to help others grows, so does my wealth.

• My day is filled with limitless abundance and love.

• I have the power to create the life I desire.

• I am happy, prosperous, and I live in abundance.

• I deserve what I desire and I receive it in abundance.

Self-Talk for Life Purpose:

- My life has meaning and purpose.

- I am clear in my purpose.

- The better I know myself, the clearer my purpose becomes.

- I matter. My life matters. Everything I do matters.

- My unique skills and talents will make a profound difference in the world.

- Today I follow my heart to discover my destiny.

- I am meant to do great things.

- I am limited only by my vision of what is possible.

- My purpose is to develop and share the best parts of myself with others.

- Today I present my love, passion, talent and joy as a gift to the world.

- I need not know the entire journey in order to take one step.

- I fulfill my life purpose by starting here and now.

- My life purpose can be whatever I decide to make it.

- I cultivate, nurture, and grow my goals

- I act with full purpose and intention

Self-Talk for Inner Peace:

• All is well, right here, right now.

• Peace begins with a conscious choice. Today I embrace that choice.

• I allow my life to be simple and peaceful.

• A peaceful heart makes for a peaceful life.

• I trust the universe to deliver me good in every situation.

• By gaining inner peace, I create peace in every experience.

• I am filled with the light of love and joy.

• I allow myself to let go. Peace comes when I let go of trying to control every tiny detail.

• I let go of stress, anxiety, and fear. Where peace dwells, fear cannot.

• Today my mission is to surrender and release.

• Peace and I are one

• I feel accepted and loved exactly as I am.

• I am strong in my weakness

• I accept everything as is.

• I am liberated from the need to be perfect

Self-Talk for Opportunity:

• Today I open my mind to opportunity.

• Opportunities are everywhere if I choose to see them.

• Endless opportunities surround me and I welcome and embrace them.

• An opportunity is only a possibility until I act on it.

• I boldly act on an opportunity when I see one.

• I give myself permission to pursue opportunities.

• I boldly go after what I want in life.

• My intuition leads me to the most lucrative opportunities.

• Opportunities are made, not found. I am working to create opportunities for myself.

• Today I see each moment as a new opportunity to express my greatness.

• I expand my awareness of the potential in each experience.

• Let each of my experiences today be a gateway to something even better.

• Each decision I make creates new opportunities.

• I adapt to changes quickly and easily to monopolize on an opportunity.

• There are no problems, only opportunities.

Self-Talk for Love:

• I attract love. I am attracting love into my life.

• I am ready for a healthy, loving relationship.

• I am worthy and deserving of love.

• All of my relationships are meaningful and fulfilling.

• As I share my love with others, the universe mirrors love back to me.

• I see everyone I meet as a soul mate.

• I trust the universe to bring the right partner who is perfect for me.

• Today I release fear and open my heart to true love.

• I am grateful for the people in my life.

• I am the perfect partner for my perfect partner.

• I deserve to be loved and I allow myself to be loved.

• Despite my fear, apprehension, and resistance, I open my heart to loving and being loved.

• I surround myself with people who accept me, care about me, and treat me well.

• I align myself with those who support me.

• I am loved.

Self-Talk for Inner Clarity:

- I have inner clarity

- I know who I am, where I am going, and what I am doing.

- Today I awaken to my higher wisdom.

- My inner voice guides me in every moment.

- I am centered, calm, and clear.

- I always know the right actions to achieve my goals.

- When I know where I'm going, getting there is a cinch!

- Today I am completely tuned in to my inner wisdom.

- Harmony is always a sign that I am balanced from within.

- Thank you for showing me the way to my dreams.

- I trust my feelings and insights.

- I am detached and open to divine guidance.

- I let go of the past, accept the present, and have faith in the future.

- I intuitively make the right decisions.

- I trust myself.

Self-Talk for Self-Love:

- I love myself.

- I accept who I am and appreciate everything about me.

- I am filled with light, love, and peace.

- I treat myself with kindness and respect.

- I don't have to be perfect; I just have to be me.

- I am me and I love it.

- I give myself permission to shine.

- I honor the best parts of myself and share the w/ others.

- I'm proud of all I have accomplished.

- Today I give myself permission to be greater than my fears.

- I love myself no matter what.

- I am my own best friend and cheerleader.

- Thank you for the qualities, traits and talents that make me so unique.

- I do loving things for myself.

- I am loved, loving, and loveable.

14329711R00045

Printed in Great Britain
by Amazon